GW01086121

Birds in the Town

Peter Gill
illustrated by the author

Published by Dinosaur Publications

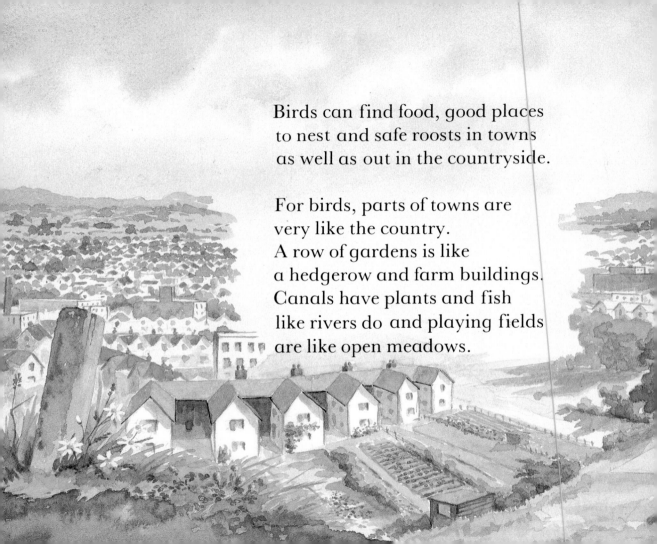

Birds can find food, good places
to nest and safe roosts in towns
as well as out in the countryside.

For birds, parts of towns are
very like the country.
A row of gardens is like
a hedgerow and farm buildings.
Canals have plants and fish
like rivers do and playing fields
are like open meadows.

Starling

Wren

Blue tit

Bullfinch

In a row of gardens, birds can find
insects and snails to eat.
There are often seeds, berries and fruit,
as well as food which people put out.
But the birds have to beware of cats.
Nest sites under roofs, in bushes and
in sheds are like those that
birds choose in the countryside.

Greenfinch
♂

Robin

Some male(♂) and female(♀) birds
look alike, but where they are different
the symbol is shown by the bird.

Song thrush

♀

♂

Blackbirds

Kingfisher

Dabchick

Pied wagtail

Coot

On the bank of the canal
a quiet fisherman
watches a pair of dabchicks.
Coots are looking for a nest site
near the water's edge.
A wren creeps among the leaves
looking for insects.
Bobbing its tail, a pied wagtail
darts for flies.
Sometimes a kingfisher flashes past or
a swan disturbs the fisherman's float.

Wren

Mute swan

Green woodpecker

In winter, flocks of migrant fieldfares
search the open grass of a school's
playing fields.
Lapwings probe the soft ground for grubs.
In the old tree at the edge of the field
a tawny owl roosts, and a treecreeper
searches the tough bark for insects.

Kestrel ♂

Swift

House martin

In the town square,
pigeons swoop down from their
perches high on buildings
to feed on the crumbs people
scatter for them.
Sparrows try to get to the food first.
Swifts and house martins wheel and
flutter above, catching
insects for their young.
A kestrel hovers, looking for
a careless sparrow.

♂ ♀
Home sparrows

Pigeon

Blue tit

Great tit ♂

Pigeon

♂ House
sparrow

Goldfinch

Wood pigeon

There are always ducks on the park lake.
Mallards live there all the year and
tufted ducks sometimes come to the
lake to feed in winter.
Swans and Canada geese on the water
and wood pigeons and feral pigeons
on the bank squabble with the ducks for
the food people throw down.
Shy moorhens get used to seeing people and
become quite brave, looking for food on the grass.
In the trees and flowerbeds
finches and tits search for
seeds and insects.

♂ Chaffinch

Moorhen

♂ Mallard

Canada goose

Tufted duck ♂

Food among the rubbish on tips
attracts many birds in winter.
Noisy gulls fight for tasty scraps.
Jackdaws are always ready to snatch a meal.
The smaller sparrows and starlings
have to wait their turn.

Magpie

Song thrush

Blue tit

Spotted
flycatcher

Birds find many kinds of food in towns.
There are insects, grubs, seeds and
fruit like those they find
out in the fields and woods.
We put food on bird tables, and they find
food that we throw away or spill.

Bullfinch ♂

Redwing

Sparrows ♂

Kestrel ♂

Birds like kestrels and tawny owls catch and eat some of the smaller birds which live or roost in the town.

Chaffinch ♂

Tawny owl

Dunnock

Lesser spotted woodpecker

Some birds nest in bushes and
holes in trees, just as they do
in the countryside.
Wagtails like holes in walls and
robins are well known for
nesting in odd places.
Others choose sites which are
similar to their usual ones.

Pied wagtail

Robin

Kestrel
♀

Kittiwakes nest on window sills which
are like ledges on a steep cliff and
gulls nest on rooftops near the sea.
Kestrels choose sites high up
on buildings and machinery.

Herring gull

Kittiwake

On cold winter nights, some birds
make for the city, where the air is
slightly warmer.
Starlings come in vast flocks
from the fields where they feed
to roost on the ledges of big buildings.
They can be a nuisance with their
noise and messy droppings.
In some cities, flocks of wagtails
gather to roost in the trees.

Buzzard

Osprey

You can see many more kinds of birds
as they pass through the town
seeking food and rest on their long
migration flights in spring and autumn.

Sand martins

Cuckoo

Golden plovers

Ducks

Others can only be heard
as they fly above,
calling to each other
to keep contact in the dark of night.

Redstart

Willow warbler

Blackcap
♂

Collared dove

Swift

Swallow

In towns, birds face extra dangers.
Cats hunt them by instinct and
rats steal their eggs.
Windows often reflect clear sky so that
fast-flying birds don't see the glass
in their way.
Poison that gardeners use to
destroy pests can kill birds too.
Birds sometimes crash into the network
of telephone wires.
Lead fishing weights swallowed by swans
and ducks slowly poison them.
It is important for us to be aware of
these hazards and to help wherever we can.

Jackdaw

Chaffinch